WORK SO HARD.

The story about Nehemiah is taken from Nehemiah 1-6.

*T*hey said to me, "Those who survived the exile and are back in the province are in great trouble and disgrace. The wall of Jerusalem is broken down, and its gates have been burned with fire."

When I heard these things, I sat down and wept. For some days I mourned and fasted and prayed before the God of heaven.

Then I said to them, "You see the trouble we are in: Jerusalem lies in ruins, and its gates have been burned with fire. Come, let us rebuild the wall of Jerusalem. . . ."

But when Sanballat the Horonite, Tobiah the Ammonite official and Geshem the Arab heard about it, they mocked and ridiculed us. "What is this you are doing?" they asked. "Are you rebelling against the king?"

I answered them by saying, "The God of heaven will give us success. We his servants will start rebuilding, but as for you, you have no share in Jerusalem or any claim or historic right to it."

Therefore I stationed some of the people behind the lowest points of the wall at the exposed places, posting

*them by families, with their swords, spears and bows. After
I looked things over, I stood up and said to the nobles, the
officials and the rest of the people, "Don't be afraid of them.
Remember the Lord, who is great and awesome, and fight for
your brothers, your sons and your daughters, your wives and
your homes."*

*So the wall was completed on the twenty-fifth of Elul, in
fifty-two days. When all our enemies heard about this, all the
surrounding nations were afraid and lost their self-confidence,
because they realised that this work had been done with the
help of our God.*

Nehemiah 1:3-4; 2:17-20; 4:13-14; 6:15-16, NIV

Why Did Nehemiah Work So Hard?

Scandinavia Publishing House
Drejervej 15,3 DK-Copenhagen NV Denmark
Tel. (+45) 3531 0330
www.scanpublishing.dk
info@scanpublishing.dk

Design by Ben Alex
Produced by Scandinavia Publishing House

Printed in China
ISBN: 9788772470429

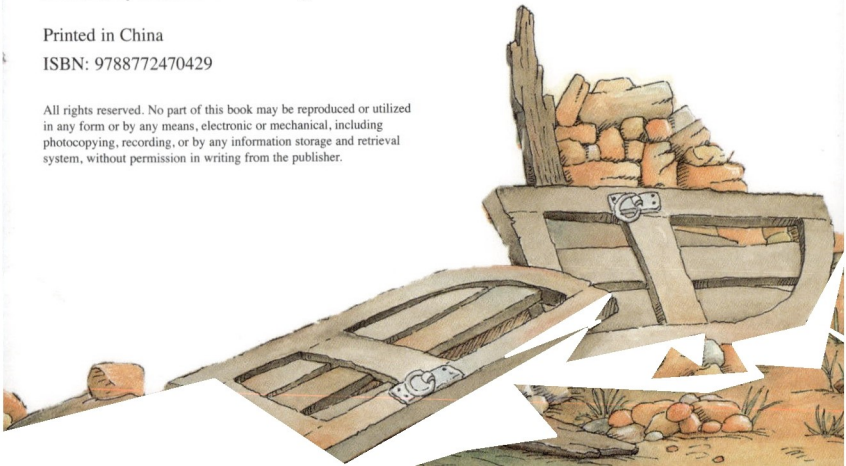

WHY DID NEHEMIAH WORK SO HARD?

By Pauline Youd

Illustrated by Elaine Garvin

SCANDINAVIA

Round and round Jerusalem Nehemiah rode. What did he see? Broken walls, burned gates, piles of broken stones everywhere.

Nehemiah cried. God's special city was in ruins. "We must rebuild the wall and make Jerusalem safe," he said.

"Yes," the people agreed. "We will rebuild the wall."
The people worked very hard.

Sanballat, Tobiah and Geshem were enemies of God. They didn't want the wall rebuilt. They laughed at Nehemiah and pointed their fingers.

"That wall is too weak," they said. "It won't hold up a little fox." But Nehemiah and the people kept building.

Sanballat, Tobiah and Geshem lied about Nehemiah.

"You just want to make yourself king of Jerusalem," they said.

"That isn't true," said Nehemiah and he kept building.

Sanballat, Tobiah and Geshem planned to attack the city. But Nehemiah prayed to God.

He gave the people weapons to protect themselves. With their weapons in one hand and ready to fight, they kept rebuilding the wall. Finally the wall was finished. Only the gates needed to be built.

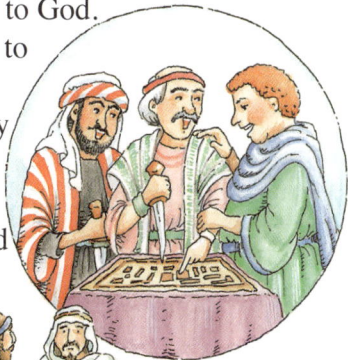

Sanballat, Tobiah and Geshem said to Nehemiah, "Can't we talk this over? Meet us outside the city."

But Nehemiah said, "No, I'm far too busy to stop and meet with you."

Then a man came and said, "Hide in the temple, Nehemiah! Sanballat, Tobiah and Geshem are going to kill you."

"I will not hide in the temple," said Nehemiah. "God will protect me while I finish the gates."

Finally, round and round Jerusalem Nehemiah rode. He saw tall, strong walls with gates.

Nehemiah and the people shouted for joy Jerusalem was safe.

Did you ever start out to do something important and then get side-tracked? You meant to keep on cleaning your room, but a friend came over. You meant to take out the garbage after lunch, but you forgot. You meant to do your homework, but you got sleepy.

In the story, Nehemiah kept on building the wall no matter what. That was what God wanted him to do. When he finished, he shouted for joy.

Learn to finish what you start. Then you'll feel happy. Just like Nehemiah!

"Don't be afraid of them. Remember the Lord, who is great and awesome, and fight for your brothers, your sons and your daughters, your wives and your homes."

Nehemiah 4:14

WONDER BOOKS
Lessons to learn from 12 Bible characters

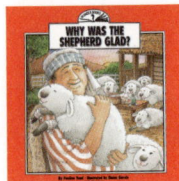

God's Love

Self-giving

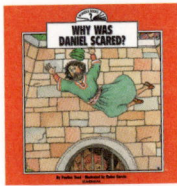

Prayer Overcomes Fear

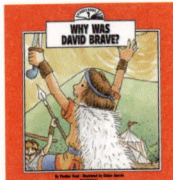

Praising God

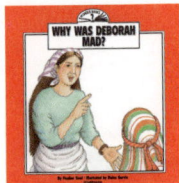

Prayer Obtains Wisdom

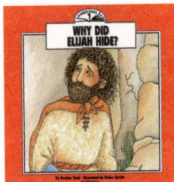

Listening to God

Trust

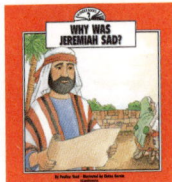

Perseverance

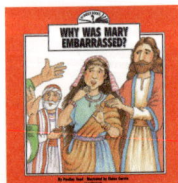

Loving Obedience

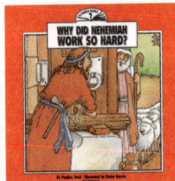

Persistence

Asking Advice

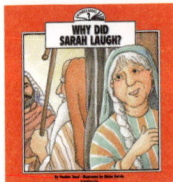

Trusting God's plan